A Kid's Guide

Climate Change

And Global Warming

Curious Kids Press • Palm Springs, CA
www.curiouskidspress.com

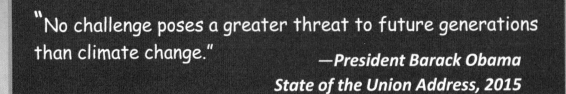

"No challenge poses a greater threat to future generations than climate change."

—President Barack Obama
State of the Union Address, 2015

Save
The Planet

SPECIAL THANKS TO:
Sybil Azur
Climate Reality Leader
Los Angeles

Publisher: Curious Kids Press, Palm Springs, CA 92264.
Designed by: Michael Owens
Editor: Sterling Moss
Copy Editor: Janice Ross PECIAL THANKS TO

Table of Contents

Climate Change:
What's the Big Deal?

A POLAR BEAR is one of the most amazing animals on the plant. It lives in one of the coldest, harshest climates on Earth—an area around the Arctic Circle, where winter temperatures can drop below –58 °F (-50 °C).

In order to survive, polar bears hunt seals. Yet, they can't catch seals in the open water. They depend on sea ice as a platform for their hunting.

Seals spend a lot of time under the sea ice, searching for food. But they are air-breathing mammals. Every once in a while, they have to come up for air. So, they make breathing holes in the ice.

Polar bears wait patiently by these breathing holes, ready to grab the seal when it pokes its head up through the ice.

Yet, recently, global warming has caused the sea ice to melt earlier in the winter and form later in the summer. It is also causing the ice to move farther from the shore. That makes it hard for polar bears to swim to the sea ice from the shore.

Global warming is making it harder for polar bears to find the food they need to survive.

Today, there are about 23,000 polar bears on Earth. If sea ice continues to melt, there will be fewer than 10,000 by 2050.

And that's a big deal.

BUT GLOBAL WARMING isn't affecting just polar bears in the Arctic. It's affecting people, places, and animals all around the world.

The tiny village of Shishmaref, Alaska, is one example. The village is located on a tiny island five miles from the mainland. It is built on permafrost (or permanently frozen ground).

In the past, summers were short and cool in Shishmaref, and winters were very, very cold. So, the ground stayed frozen.

In recent years, however, the temperature in Shishmaref has gotten warmer and warmer. The permafrost is starting to thaw during the summer months. As much as 23 feet (seven meters) of Shishmaref's shoreline washes into the sea each year. One day the people of Shishmaref may lose their village entirely.

And that's a big deal.

THE SEA LEVEL AROUND THE WORLD IS RISING. Almost all the rise is the result of global warming. Global warming affects sea level in two ways. First, global warming warms oceans. Warmer water expands (takes up more room). Secondly, global warming causes glaciers and sea ice to melt, dumping tons of extra water into the oceans.

What does that mean for cities and countries around the world? A rise in global temperature of only 2 degrees Celsius could spell disaster for many coastal cities around the world. It could leave portions of the world's coastal cities—and some smaller countries—underwater.

The Maldives, an island nation in the Indian Ocean, is one. If global warming continues at the present rate, the Maldives will be under water by 2030.

But that's not all. The salty seawater could harm or damage crops. It could also contaminate drinking water. And, as the sea level rises, it could threaten wildlife populations, such as the sea turtles, who make their home on the beaches.

And all of that is a very big deal.

If all the glaciers in the world suddenly melted, the earth's oceans would rise 230 feet (70 meters). Of course, that's unlikely to happen any time soon. But if it did, the Statue of Liberty in the New York Harbor would be underwater. It's only 151 feet (46 meters) tall.

THESE ARE JUST a few examples of what's happening around the world as the result of global warming. There are many more.

Today, politicians, scientists, teachers, and especially young people are all looking to find solutions to climate change. You can help, too.

The first step is to learn as much as you can about climate change and global warming—what it is, what causes it, and what can be done to help prevent it.

That's what this book is all about.

Working together on a solution to climate change can help keep the planet safe for the future. It may even help save the tiny village of Shishmaref, or even the magnificent polar bears of the Arctic.

WHaT IS GLoBaL WaRMiNG?

Quick Answer: Global warming is the increase in the average surface temperature of Earth over time.

Climate Change

Global Warming

PEOPLE OFTEN USE THE TERMS "global warming" and "climate change" to mean the same thing. But there's a difference.

When we talk about global warming, we are talking about the fact that the earth's temperature is getting warmer over long periods of time, 30 years or more.

When we talk about climate change, on the other hand, we are talking about the effects or results of global warming. Global warming causes such things as rising sea levels, shrinking mountain glaciers, stronger and more frequent storms, and even a change in when plants and flowers bloom. All those things are part of climate change.

THERE'S ONE OTHER THING to know about the term global warming. The term is usually used to talk about warming that results from human activity—things like driving a car or throwing away plastic water bottles. Both of those things contribute to global warming. You'll read more about those things later in this book.

No matter what term you use, though, the problem is a serious one. Many experts estimate that the average temperature will rise an additional 2.5 to 10.4 degrees F (1.4 to 5.8 degrees C) by 2100. That could spell disaster for the planet. Many plants and animals could become extinct. Life on Earth as we know it could change dramatically and become much more difficult for everyone.

97% of climate scientists agree that humans are the main cause of global warming and climate change.

In the past, it took the planet 5,000 years to heat up 5 degrees Celsius. Many scientists believe the planet could heat up another 5 degrees Celsius in less than 100 years.

Years ago, there were 150 glaciers in Montana's Glacier National Park. Today, there are only 25 glaciers bigger than 25 acres left.

Weather or Climate: What's the Difference?

HOW'S THE WEATHER?

It's a question we all ask all the time. Is it cold and raining? Is it sunny and hot!

Those are *weather* conditions. They tell us what the weather is like over a short period of time, usually only hours or maybe days. Rain, snow, wind, hurricanes, tornadoes—these are all weather events.

Climate is different. It refers to weather conditions in a place or region over many years, usually 30 years or more.

In Minneapolis in winter, it is usually cold and snowy. That's the climate of Minneapolis. The climate tells about typical conditions in an area that are fairly consistent over long periods of time. Each part of the world has its own climate.

How's the weather in your city today? What's the climate like?

The view across frozen Lake Calhoun in Minneapolis, MN.

Why is the Earth Heating Up?

GLOBAL WARMING

ON JULY 4, 2019, the temperature at Anchorage (Alaska) International airport reached 90 degrees Fahrenheit (90°F)—an all-time high. The average temperature in Anchorage during summer months is normally only in the mid-sixties!

The "heat-wave" in Anchorage that July day probably didn't surprise a lot of climate scientists. Since the 1950s, Alaska has been warming twice as fast as the global average. Simply put, record-breaking high temperatures across Alaska today are not uncommon.

But what is causing this change in temperature in Anchorage and many other parts of the world? The answer is not always easy and is often complex.

Many climate scientists believe that human activity—the things we humans do on a day-to-day basis like driving a car—is one of the big causes of global warming.

Before reading more about the causes of global warming, it's important to understand something called "the greenhouse effect."

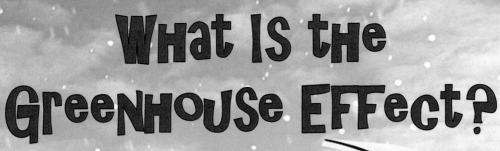

What Is the Greenhouse Effect?

HAVE YOU EVER VISITED a greenhouse in winter? A greenhouse is a building with glass walls and a glass roof. It is used to grow fruits, flowers, and other plants in the wintertime.

How does it work? Rays of sunlight pass through the glass walls and ceiling of the greenhouse. The glass of the greenhouse traps the heat and prevents much of it from leaving. As a result, the greenhouse stays warm all winter long, helping the plants grow.

In some ways, our planet is like a greenhouse. Certain gases, known as greenhouse gases, keep heat from escaping into the atmosphere. They help our planet stay a warm and cozy 58 degrees Fahrenheit (14 degrees Celsius), on average.

That's a good thing. Without greenhouse gases in the atmosphere, the average temperature on Earth would be 0 °F (-18 °C). Pretty scary.

But what happens if the greenhouse effect becomes stronger? It could trap too much heat and make the earth dangerously warm. Even a little extra warming may cause problems for humans, plants, and animals in the future.

Did You Know?

There are a number of different greenhouse gases in the atmosphere. The two most common are carbon dioxide (CO_2) and methane (CH_4).

CO_2 enters the atmosphere mainly through burning of fossil fuels (oil, gas, and coal).

CH_4 enters the atmosphere from deforestation and from livestock and other agricultural practices.

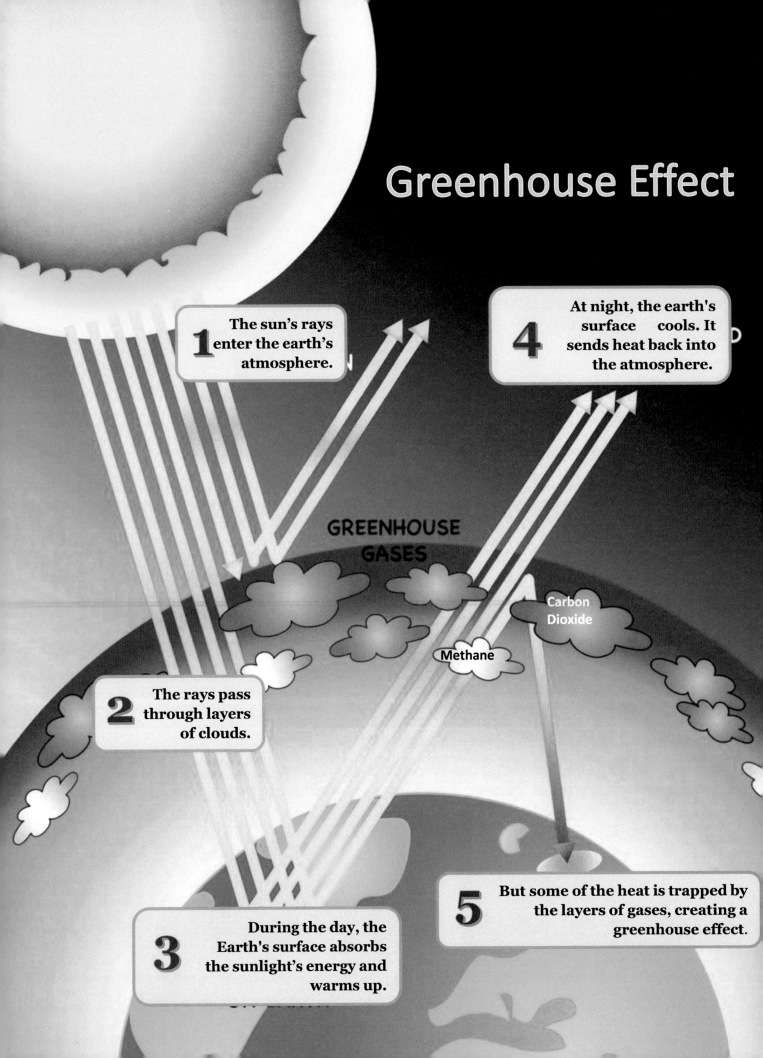

Greenhouse Effect

1 The sun's rays enter the earth's atmosphere.

4 At night, the earth's surface cools. It sends heat back into the atmosphere.

GREENHOUSE GASES

Carbon Dioxide

Methane

2 The rays pass through layers of clouds.

5 But some of the heat is trapped by the layers of gases, creating a greenhouse effect.

3 During the day, the Earth's surface absorbs the sunlight's energy and warms up.

Fossils and Forests and Cows, Oh, My!

What Causes Greenhouse Gases?

YOU MIGHT BE WONDERING, "Where do all those greenhouse gases come from?"

Some greenhouse gases occur naturally in the environment. Carbon dioxide, for example, is a natural part of the earth's atmosphere.

But carbon dioxide and other greenhouse gases are also created by human activity. In the past 150 years, greenhouse gases in the atmosphere have increased dramatically. Human activities have been the main reason for that increase.

So, what are some of the human activities that cause greenhouse gases? Burning fossil fuels is a big one. But deforestation (the cutting down of trees) also adds greenhouse gas to the atmosphere. And, then, there's livestock. Believe it or not, cows (and other livestock) make a major contribution to the problem. Read more about each of these sources of greenhouse gas on the next pages.

Fossil Fuels and Global Warming

SO, WHAT ARE FOSSIL FUELS, anyway?

The short answer is fuel, such as coal, oil, or gas, that comes from fossils.

Fossils are the remains of plants and animals that lived long ago. Over time, the bones and shells and other matter from the remains were buried deep in the ground. The heat and pressure of being so far under the earth changed them. They became coal, oil, and gas.

Here are some other facts about fossil fuels:

- It took a long time for fossil fuels to develop. The fossil fuels we use today began forming long before dinosaurs roamed the earth.

- Fossil fuels in their natural form cannot be made by humans.

- Fossil fuels are "non-renewable." That means once the world runs out of fossil fuels, there are no more.

Today, we burn these fossil fuels for many things. For example:

- Fossil fuels, such as coal, are used by power plants to produce electricity.

- Fossil fuels are used to make gasoline and other fuel for cars, trucks, ships, trains, and planes .

- Fossil fuels are used to heat homes and to cook in kitchens.

How much fossil fuel is left in the world? It's hard to say. The best guess is that we have enough fossil fuels to last about another 115 years, give or take a decade or so.

But that could change over time. It depends on whether there is an increase or decrease in fossil fuels in the world.

The largest source of greenhouse gas from human activities is from burning fossil fuels for electricity, heat, and transportation.

Cows and Global Warming

DO CHEESEBURGERS contribute to global warming?

Some people think so. That may seem strange, but here's why.

All cows (and other livestock like sheep and goats) emit (or give off) methane, a greenhouse gas. How? Mostly through belching (though passing gas also sends a smaller amount of methane into the air).

Today, there are more than 1.5 billion cows in the world. That's a lot of belching. And a lot of methane.

In fact, almost half of all methane that's produced by agriculture comes from livestock.

So, the idea is: Cut down on cheeseburgers (and other meat products) and you cut down on the need for beef cattle, which cuts down on methane.

That doesn't mean that everyone needs to become a vegetarian. But cutting down on the amount of meat people eat (including cheeseburgers) could help cut down on global warming.

In the meantime, scientists, farmers, and others are looking for ways to reduce the level of methane from livestock. For example, cows that are raised on grain produce less greenhouse gas than cows that graze on grass.

Did You Know?
Americans eat 50 BILLION burgers a year. That's three burgers a week for every man, woman, and kid!

Excuse me while I burp methane.

Forests and Global Warming

IN 2018, THE WORLD LOST 30 million acres of trees through deforestation. That's roughly the size of the state of New York.

Why is that important?

Trees play an important role in the fight against global warming. They absorb (take in) carbon dioxide from the atmosphere, store it in the soil, and use it to make their own food.

When trees are cut down, they release all of the carbon dioxide that they are storing back into the atmosphere.

Deforestation (the removal of forests or trees from an area of land) is a major cause of global warming. In fact, today, deforestation adds more carbon dioxide into the atmosphere than all the cars and trucks on the world's roads and highways.

Deforestation is often the result of wildfires. But some cattle farmers also contribute to deforestation. They cut down trees to make more room for raising cattle or planting crops.

Wildfires in the Amazon Rainforest
In 2019, more than 75,000 wildfires raged through the Amazon rainforest in Brazil. That was more than double the number of wildfires in that area the previous year.

Does Plastic Affect Global Warming?

The Short Answer: Yes. Greenhouse gases are emitted (or sent out) at all stages in the lifecycle of plastic—starting with its production from fossil fuels to its disposal in landfills.

THINK ABOUT ALL THE WAYS you use plastic. Plastic straws. Plastic grocery bags. Plastic water bottles—lots of plastic water bottles. In fact, Americans use more than two and a half million plastic bottes EVERY HOUR.

Now think about what happens to all those plastic items, often after being used only once.

Some of it is recycled, for sure. But not much. Most of it ends up in landfills like this one. There, it sits with the hot sun beating down on it for hundreds of years as the plastic breaks down into smaller and smaller pieces.

As the plastic breaks down, it gives off both carbon dioxide and methane in about equal amounts. But methane is much more effective at trapping heat in the atmosphere over a long period of time—as much as 36 times more effective.

So, what can be done to prevent these plastic landfills from contributing to global warming?

There's an easy answer: SAY NO TO SINGLE-USE PLASTIC.

Cut back on the number of bottles, bags, plastic straws, and other plastics you use every day. Take your old plastic and paper bags back to the grocery store for reuse or recycling. And reuse plastic bottles whenever you can.

It won't solve the problem. But by reducing your plastics "footprint," you can reduce your carbon footprint. And that's a good thing.

WHat'S YouR CaRBoN FootpRiNt?

Quick Answer:

The amount of carbon dioxide (and other greenhouse gases) a person releases (or puts) into the atmosphere during a year, based on his or her activities during the year.

EVERY KID IN THE WORLD (and every adult, too) has a carbon footprint.

It's not a footprint you can see, like a footprint in the wet sand at the beach. But it's a very important footprint.

So, what is a carbon footprint? It's the total amount of carbon dioxide people create in your daily activities. Whenever we burn fossil fuels, such as coal, oil, and natural gas, we are causing carbon dioxide to enter the atmosphere.

Many scientists say that today people throughout the world are putting too much carbon dioxide into the atmosphere. How!

You can read about three of those ways on the next page. Then, just for fun, take a quick quiz to see just how "green" you are.

Transportation

Cars create a lot of carbon dioxide. Even a 2-mile car trip puts 2 pounds of CO_2 into the atmosphere! Whenever you ride in a car, you are adding to your carbon footprint.

Electricity

But the biggest way people add to their carbon footprint is through electricity. Electricity itself doesn't create carbon dioxide. But the power plants that produce the electricity do.

Trash

The trash you create during the day also adds to your carbon footprint. Over time, trash produces carbon dioxide.

So, whenever you play a video game or run your computer, you are contributing to your personal carbon footprint.

It's impossible today to totally eliminate a person's carbon footprint. But the goal should be to make your carbon footprint as small as possible. There are many ways to do that. You can read about some of them on page 32.

AN Imaginary Interview With a CLiMate ScieNtist

Here are some questions kids ask most about global warming and climate change.

I read that only about 8 percent of all the sea ice in the Arctic has melted in the last 30 years. That doesn't seem like much.

Tell that to the polar bears and the seals that depend on sea ice for their survival. The fact is 8 percent means that an area of ice the size of Norway, Sweden, and Denmark (or Texas and Arizona) combined has now disappeared.

Do volcanoes emit more carbon dioxide than human activity?

Good question. Lots of people think that. But the answer is no. Not nearly as much. Let me give you an example. The eruption of Mount St. Helens in 1980 sent 10 million tons of carbon dioxide into the atmosphere in just nine hours. Humans release about the same amount of CO2 in 2 1/2 hours.

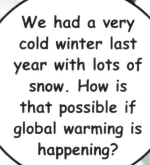

We had a very cold winter last year with lots of snow. How is that possible if global warming is happening?

Sometimes a city or town will have a colder than usual winter. Other times, it may have a hotter than usual summer. Neither one, by itself, is the result of global warming or no global warming. Climate change is a long-term problem.

Why do some people not believe in global warming and climate change?

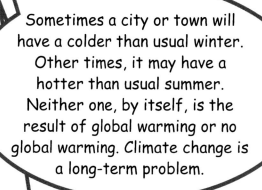

Probably a couple of reasons. First, the pace of global warming is slow. It's not something that happens overnight. But also people think about climate change in terms of their local weather, rather than global trends.

What Might Happen If the Earth Keeps Getting Warmer?

THE PLANET is warming up fast...real fast. Since 1900, in fact, the planet's average surface temperature rose about 1.62 degrees Fahrenheit (0.9 degrees Celsius)!

That doesn't seem like much, does it? It's less than two degrees Fahrenheit over more than 100 years.

Yet, many climate scientists say the average temperature of Earth doesn't have to get too much warmer to cause severe problems. An increase of only 3.2 degrees Fahrenheit (1.8 degrees Celsius) or less could do it.

So, what are the problems that might occur with global warming?

You can read about some of them on the next page.

"If humanity does nothing about climate change, rising temperatures [and] extreme weather could end up triggering a global food crisis."

—United Nations on Climate Change

Here are just a few of the things that many scientists say may happen as the result of global warming.

Event	WHAT'S EXPECTED	WHAT COULD HAPPEN	WHY IT MATTERS
Rising Temperature	Earth's temperature could increase by as much as 8.5°F (4.8°C) over the next few decades.	An increase in both floods and droughts and other severe weather	World food supply and fresh water could be reduced; certain diseases, such as malaria or asthma, could increase.
Melting Sea Ice	Summer sea ice may disappear by 2050.	Polar bears who need ice as a platform to hunt for food (namely seals) are likely to become extinct in parts of Alaska and Canada.	Many organisms are connected to polar bears via a food web. For example, without polar bears the seal population would increase. That would decrease fish that seals feed on.
Retreating Glaciers	All the alpine glaciers in the world will continue to lose mass and thickness.	The availability of fresh water could dry up. Natural hazards, such as landslides and avalanches could happen more often.	Nearly two BILLION people in the world get their water and power from glaciers. Remove the glaciers and the water supply will dry up.
Thawing Permafrost	With every 1°C increase in temperature, 1.5 million square miles of permafrost could be lost.	When permafrost warms and thaws, it releases carbon dioxide and methane into the air.	Carbon dioxide and methane are greenhouse gases that trap heat from escaping into the atmosphere.
Rising Sea Level	By the year 2100, our oceans will be one to four feet higher.	Low-lying areas, such as Miami, FL, as well as whole countries could experience severe flooding. Sea water will seep into fresh water sources in the ground.	Millions of people will lose their homes, if not their lives. Many coastal areas rely on freshwater sources for their drinking water. Also, many forms of wildlife, such as the sea turtle, may find their habitats damaged by flooding.

The Year 2050
What's at Stake?

Global warming could affect people and the environment in many different ways. Here are just some of them.

What's at Stake?

HEALTH

Global warming can result in illnesses, caused by heat waves, including heat cramps, heat stroke, and even death. In fact, heat waves cause more deaths in the United States every year than hurricanes, tornadoes, floods, and earthquakes combined.

What's at Stake?

AGRICULTURE

Global warming could make it too hot to grow certain crops in some areas and could cause droughts in other areas. As a result, our food supply could be reduced.

What's at Stake?

ENERGY

Hotter days mean people will use their air conditioning more, which means using more electricity. The use of more electricity, which is produced by burning fossil fuels, means more greenhouse gases will be added to the atmosphere.

What's at Stake?

WATER SUPPLY

Many places rely on snowmelt to fill the lakes, rivers, and streams that help keep drinking water reservoirs full and provide water to irrigate crops. Warmer weather means less snow which means less snowmelt which means less water flowing into rivers and lakes.

What's at Stake?

PLANTS, ANIMALS, ECOSYSTEMS

Many plants and animals, such as polar bears, need to live in cold environments. If the earth keeps getting warmer, up to one–fourth of all the plants and animals on Earth could become extinct within 100 years.

What's at Stake?

COASTAL AREAS

Global warming can cause sea levels to rise, putting cities like Miami, Florida or Venice, Italy, at risk of flooding or worse.

What's at Stake?

RECREATION

Global warming can affect both summertime and wintertime activities. As temperatures rise, there may be shorter seasons for cold weather sports like skiing or ice skating, or snowmobiling. At the same time, rising sea levels could wash away many beaches.

What's at Stake?

FORESTS

Global warming could cause an increase in droughts and extremely dry conditions, resulting in more wildfires in the forests and grasslands around the world. Just a one- to two-degree increase in global temperature can lead to a much greater risk of wildfires.

The Next Chapter
Renewable Energy

MOST OF THE ELECTRICITY that powers our homes in the U.S. and other parts of the world is produced in power plants. How? Here's the short answer.

1. The power plants burn fossil fuels (coal or oil) to heat water.
2. The hot water produces steam.
3. The steam turns a windmill-like machine called a turbine.
4. The turbine is part of a machine called a generator.
5. The generator turns the energy from the rotating turbine into electricity.

The trouble is that burning fuels like coal and oil sends carbon dioxide into the atmosphere. And that adds to global warming.

So an important question is: "Is it possible to produce electricity without producing more carbon dioxide?"

And the answer is "Yes, we can!"

There are several ways to do that. But two of the easiest to understand are the sun and the wind.

Wind power is energy that is generated directly from the wind.

Solar power is energy that comes directly from sunlight.

These sources of energy are called clean energy or renewable energy? Why?

They are clean energy because they do not produce greenhouse gases. And they are renewable energy sources because we'll never run out of sun and wind.

Today, only about one-fourth of the world's power comes from clean, renewable energy. Many scientists say that by using more renewable energy to power our lives in the future, we will help the planet survive.

This wind farm produces clean energy through the use of wind turbines.

HOW Green Are You? Take This Quiz to Find Out!

HOW GREEN ARE YOU? The answer to that has a lot to do with the activities you do each day. Those activities contribute to your carbon footprint.

To get an accurate measurement of your carbon footprint is complicated. But this quiz can help get you started. Once you know what your carbon footprint looks like, you can start taking steps to shrink it down to size, if you need to.

How Green Are You? Quiz

Direction: Read each question. Put an X on the space that best answers the question.

1. How do you usually get to and from school?

_____a. Ride in car with parents or friends.

_____b. Take a bus

_____c. Walk or ride bike

2. How often do you eat meat for dinner?

_____a. 5-7 nights a week

_____b. 3-4 nights a week

_____c. 1-2 nights a week

3. When not using your computer or charging your cell phone, do you...

_____a. leave it plugged in?

_____b. power down?

_____c. unplug it?

4. How often do you recycle and/or reuse?

_____a. Never

_____b. Sometimes

_____c. Always

---

5. Whenever you're thirsty for water, do you...

____a. grab a new plastic bottle of water?

____b. grab a new plastic bottle of water but plan to talk with your parents about alternatives to plastic bottles.

____c. use a refillable water bottle?

6. When you buy one or two small items at a grocery store or deli, do you...

____a. ask for a plastic bag to put the items in?

____b. put them in a bag you brought in with you?

____c. carry them out by hand or put them in a reusable bag you brought with you?

7. When you brush your teeth, do you let the water run?

____a. Yes

____b. Sometimes

____c. No, never.

8. How often do you recycle?

____a. Never

____ b. Sometimes

____ c. Always

What's Your Score?

Now total up your score. Give yourself one point for every "a" answer, two points for every "b" answer, and 3 points for every "c" answer. Then, look at the Going Green Chart. How's your carbon footprint?

Going Green Chart

6-9: Think about ways you can reduce your carbon footprint

10-14: Not bad. You're definitely headed in the right direction.

15-18: CONGRATULATIONS! You're really "going green"!

Fight Global Warming
7 Things You Can Do

Fight back!

GLOBAL WARMING is a huge problem and one that adults in countries around the world will have to work together to solve.

But kids can help, too. There are many things we all can do to help slow down global warming. Here are eight of them.

PLANT A TREE: Planting a tree is one of the best ways to combat global warming. Trees help remove carbon dioxide from the atmosphere. It is also one of the cheapest and easiest ways to help the fight against global warming.

Living Green Tip: Not all trees are equal. Certain pine trees, oak trees, and Douglas fir trees are particularly good at absorbing and storing carbon dioxide.

BIKE OR WALK TO SCHOOL: Even a 2-mile car trip puts 2 pounds of CO_2 into the atmosphere!

Living Green Tip: Stay out of the drive-thru at fast-food restaurants as often as you can. Instead, park and walk inside. Without the car's engine running, you can cut down on pollution.

EAT LESS MEAT: Cows and other livestock produce about 15% of global greenhouse gases. That's as much as all the cars, trains, ships, and planes on the planet produce.

Living Green Tip: You don't have to give up cheeseburgers altogether. Add just a couple of meatless meals to your diet each week and you can make a big dent in your carbon footprint.

LET IT ROT: Composting is a fun (and easy) way to keep food waste and other items out of landfills, which, in turn, cuts down on greenhouse gas emissions.

Living Green Tip: Keep a compost pail in the kitchen and put coffee grounds, tea bags, apple cores, vegetable scraps, eggshells, nut shells, and stale bread in it (among other things). Then, dump the contents of the pail in into a compost tumbler after dinner each night. Add a little water and rotate once a week. In about four to six weeks, you'll have turned waste into fresh soil ready for vegetable seeds and you'll have helped cut down on greenhouse gas, too!

TAKE A SHOWER: Filling the bathtub uses up to 70 gallons of water, while a 5-minute shower only uses 10 to 25 gallons of water.

Living Green Tip: Take short showers rather than a bath when you can.

SPREAD THE WORD: Talk with your family and friends about global warming and why it's important. Write a letter to people in the U.S. government and encourage them to work to help reduce global warming.

Living Green Tip: Talk with your teacher about the idea of hosting a Green Planet Education Day at your school. Brainstorm with your class about global warming activities, posters, experiments, and even YouTube videos you can create for your Green Planet Day.

TURN OFF, UNPLUG, SHUT DOWN: You might be surprised to learn that all electronics use energy EVEN IF they're powered down. So, although your device isn't charging, you're still contributing to your carbon footprint.

Living Green Tip: Plug your electronic devices (cell phones, tablets, laptops) into a surge protector or power strip that has an on/off switch. Then you can shut off all the power without unplugging each gadget.

Reduce, Reuse, Recycle?

CUT DOWN ON TRASH: Trash in landfills is a disaster for the environment. It is also the third leading cause of methane (a greenhouse gas) being released in the atmosphere in the U.S.

Living Green Tip: You can cut down on trash by following the three R's: reduce, reuse, recycle. Here are some things you can recycle.

Is It Too Late to Stop Global Warming?

Teenage Climate Activist Greta Thunberg Says "No"

ON AUGUST 20, 2018, a young girl from Sweden named Greta Thunberg decided to skip school. She wanted to protest global warming. She made a sign that read "Skolstrejk förklimatet" (school strike for climate). Then, she sat outside the Swedish parliament with her sign.

At first, she sat alone. But by the second day, other people who heard about her "strike" joined her. Soon, she became known around the world for her protest against global warming.

In April 2019, Greta spoke to the British Parliament in London, England. She talked about how climate change threatens the future of the planet. But she also expressed hope.

"I'm sure that the moment we start behaving as if we are in an emergency," she said, "we can avoid a climate and ecological catastrophe. Humans are very adaptable; we can still fix this. But the opportunity to do so will not last for long. We must start today."

Many people—young and old—have been inspired by Greta's determination to bring attention to climate change. They, too, are demanding we start today to end global warming.

Photo Credit: Anders Hellberg

Greta Thunberg stands in front of the Swedish Parliament with her sign that reads "School strike for the climate."

"The climate crisis is both the easiest and the hardest issue we have ever faced. The easiest because we know what we must do."

—Greta Thunberg, Teenage Climate Activist

Glossary

Arctic Circle: An imaginary line drawn around the earth parallel to the equator and south of the North Pole.

Atmosphere: The layer of air surrounding the earth that protects us from the sun's rays.

Carbon dioxide (CO2): A type of gas in the atmosphere that traps energy from the sun.

Carbon footprint: The sum of all emissions of CO2 (carbon dioxide) caused by an individual's activities in a given time period, usually a year.

Deforestation: The act of cutting down or burning all trees within a certain area.

Emissions: Substances put into the air, such as fumes from an automobile.

Fossil Fuels: Oil and gas that form when organic matter (the remains of once-living things) is buried under great pressure and heated over millions of years.

Glacier: Huge, thick mass of ice that forms from snowfall over many centuries and moves slowing across a land surface.

Global warming: An increase in the average temperature of the earth's atmosphere over time.

Greenhouse effect: Warming of the earth as the result of sun's rays being trapped by certain gases, such as carbon dioxide.

Mammal: A vertebrate animal that produces live young as opposed to laying eggs.

Methane (CH4): A type of gas in the atmosphere that traps energy from the sun.

Natural gas: A common fossil fuel source that comes from methane gas.

Permafrost: Permanently frozen ground.

Petroleum: A liquid that comes from oil. We put it into our cars to make them run.

Sea ice: Frozen ocean water.

Resources

The following resources were consulted in the writing of this book.

WEB SITES

Climate.gov
NOAA Climate.gov is a source of timely and authoritative scientific data and information about climate.

https://www.climate.gov/

The Center for Climate and Energy Solutions (C2ES)
(formerly the Pew Center on Global Climate Change)
An independent organization working to forge practical solutions to climate change.
https://www.c2es.org/

The Intergovernmental Panel on Climate Change (IPCC)
The United Nations body for assessing the science related to climate change.
https://www.ipcc.ch/

National Academy of Sciences (NAC)
A private, nonprofit organization of the country's leading researchers.
http://www.nasonline.org/

National Aeronautics and Space Administration (NASA)
"NASA Global Climate Change: Vital Signs of the Planet"
https://climate.nasa.gov/

National Oceanic and Atmospheric Administration (NOAA)
Mission: To understand and predict changes in climate, weather, oceans and coasts.
https://www.noaa.gov/

United States Environmental Protection Agency (EPA)
The mission of the EPA is to protect human health and the environment.
https://www.epa.gov/

United States Geological Survey (USGS)
USGS is the sole science agency for the Department of the Interior.
https://www.usgs.gov/

ARTICLES

"All About Frozen Ground"
National Snow and Ice Data Center (NSIDC)
https://nsidc.org/cryosphere/frozenground/climate.html

"Climate Change Impacts"
February 2019
NOAA
https://www.noaa.gov/education/resource-collections/climate-education-resources/climate-change-impacts

"Climate Change: The Results of Disappearing Glacier"
Glacier National Park
https://www.nps.gov/glac/learn/nature/climate-change.htm

"Deforestation and Its Extreme Effect on Global Warming"
Scientific American
https://www.scientificamerican.com/article/deforestation-and-global-warming/

"Gassy Cows Are Warming the Planet, and They're Here to Stay"
National Public Radio
https://www.npr.org/sections/thesalt/2014/04/11/301794415/gassy-cows-are-warming-the-planet-and-theyre-here-to-stay

"Global Warming"
Food and Agriculture Organization of the United Nations
http://www.fao.org/3/u8480e/U8480E0y.htm

"Here's What 250 Feet of Sea Level Rise Looks Like"
The Weather Channel
https://weather.com/science/environment/news/sea-level-rise-climate-change-maps-jeffrey-linn

"New Report Highlights Increasing Risks to Coastal Homes from Sea Level Rise and Storms"
The Union of Concerned Scientists
https://www.ucsusa.org/about-us

"Overview of Greenhouse Gases"
EPA
https://www.epa.gov/ghgemissions/overview-greenhouse-gases

"Overview: Weather, Global Warming and Climate Change"
Global Climate Change
NASA
https://climate.nasa.gov/resources/global-warming-vs-climate-change/

"Plastics = Climate Change"
Below 2°C
https://below2c.org/2019/07/plastic-climate-change/

"Sea Level Rise"
Smithsonian/Ocean Portal Team
https://ocean.si.edu/through-time/ancient-seas/sea-level-rise

"Sources of Greenhouse Gas Emissions"
EPA
https://www.epa.gov/ghgemissions/sources-greenhouse-gas-emissions

"Special Report: Global Warming of 1.5°C"
IPCC
https://www.ipcc.ch/sr15/

"Sweeping New Report on Global Environmental Impact of Plastics Reveals Severe Damage to Climate"
Center for International Environmental Law
https://www.ciel.org/news/plasticandclimate/

"The Hard Truths of Climate Change—By the Numbers"
Nature: International Journal of Science
https://www.nature.com/

"Volcanoes Can Affect the Earth's Climate"
USGS
https://volcanoes.usgs.gov/vhp/gas_climate.html

"What's the Difference Between Global Warming and Climate Change"
NOAA https://www.climate.gov/news-features/climate-qa/whats-difference-between-global-warming-and-climate-change

BOOKS

Henson, Robert. *The Thinking Person's Guide to Climate Change: Second Edition.* Boston, MA: American Meteorological Society, 2019.

Romm, Joseph, Ph.D. *Climate Change: What Everyone Needs to Know.* New York, NY: Oxford University Press, Second Edition, 2018.

Wallace-Wells, David. *The Uninhabitable Earth: Life After Warming.* New York, NY: Tim Duggan Books, Crown Publishing Group, 2019.

Explore the World

Find these books on Amazon.com
Preview them at curiouskidspress.com

A Kid's Guide to AUSTRALIA

A Kid's Guide to KENYA

A Kid's Guide to France

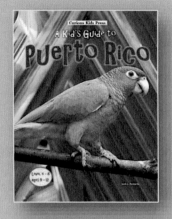

A Kid's Guide to Puerto Rico

A Kid's Guide to CHINA

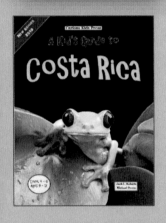

A Kid's Guide to Costa Rica

A Kid's Guide to England

A Kid's Guide to THAILAND

A Kid's Guide to SOUTH AMERICA

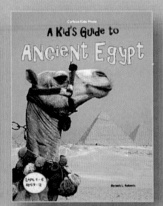

A Kid's Guide to ANCIENT EGYPT

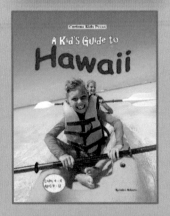

A Kid's Guide to Hawaii

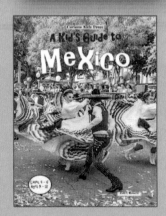

A Kid's Guide to MEXICO

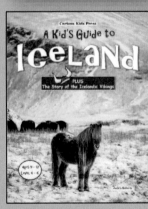

A Kid's Guide to ICELAND
PLUS
The Story of the Icelandic Vikings

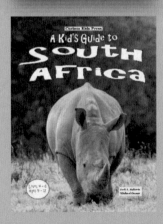

A Kid's Guide to SOUTH AFRICA

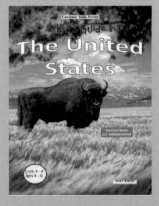

A Kid's Guide to The United States

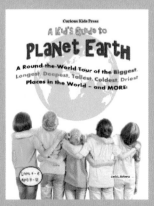

A Kid's Guide to PLANET EARTH
A Round-the-World Tour of the Biggest,
Longest, Deepest, Tallest, Coldest, Driest
Places in the World – and MORE!

About the Authors

Jack L. Roberts began his career in educational publishing at Children's Television Workshop (now Sesame Workshop), where he was Senior Editor of The Sesame Street/Electric Company Reading Kits. Later, at Scholastic Inc., he was the founding editor of a high-interest/low-reading level magazine for middle school students. He also founded two technology magazines for teachers and administrators.

Roberts is the author of more than two dozen biographies and other nonfiction books for young readers, published by Scholastic Inc., the Lerner Publishing Group, Teacher Created Materials, Benchmark Education, and others. More recently, he was the co-founder of WordTeasers, an educational series of card decks designed to help kids of all ages improve their vocabulary through "conversation, not memorization."

Michael Owens is a noted jazz dance teacher, award-winning wildlife photographer, graphic arts designer, and devoted animal lover.

In 2017, Roberts and Owens launched Curious Kids Press (CKP), an educational publishing company focused on publishing high-interest, nonfiction books for young readers, primarily books about countries and cultures around the world. Currently, CKP has published two series of country books: "A Kid's Guide to . . ." (for ages 9-12) and "Let's Visit . . ." (for ages 6-8) — both designed to help young readers explore the wonderful world of diversity in everything from food and holidays to geography and traditions.

Made in the USA
Monee, IL
04 December 2019